THERE IS
A CONDITION

RECOGNISING THE CONDITIONS
OF SUCCESSFUL LIFE

THERE IS
A CONDITION

RECOGNISING THE CONDITIONS
OF SUCCESSFUL LIFE

Maxwell Kobina Acquah
(YEFULKAY)

TATE PUBLISHING
AND **ENTERPRISES**, LLC

Published by Tate Publishing & Enterprises, LLC
127 E. Trade Center Terrace | Mustang, Oklahoma 73064 USA
1.888.361.9473 | www.tatepublishing.com

Tate Publishing is committed to excellence in the publishing industry. The company reflects the philosophy established by the founders, based on Psalm 68:11,
"The Lord gave the word and great was the company of those who published it."

Book design copyright © 2015 by Tate Publishing, LLC. All rights reserved.

Published in the United States of America

ISBN: 978-1-63268-545-2
1. Philosophy / Ethics & Moral Philosophy
2. Philosophy / General
14.11.05

Reviews:

"There is A Condition" author Maxwell Kobina Acquah's reminder to both believers of YHWH (Jehovah) and invitation to non-believers to reflect upon the principles of:

1) "So whatever you wish that others would do to you, do also to them, for this is the Law and the Prophets." (Matt 7:12)
2) But seek first the kingdom of God and his righteousness, and all these things will be added to you.

The book is organised in an easy to read manner, of which the author will first cite the scriptures, prior to expounding upon the principles embedded within the Bible.

The said condition is surprisingly simple to comprehend, yet if based on mere mortal efforts, absolutely difficult to attain. However the good news is found in the following verse "What is impossible with man is possible with God." (Luke 18:27).

"There Is A Condition" can be completed leisurely under an hour. It has my recommendation to both believers and non-believers. Thank you brother Maxwell for the reminder!

Reviewed by Amos Rao -
sg.linkedin.com/in/amosrao
www.cnbossa.org & www.bossainternship.org

Understanding God's principles and man's responsibilities, said by Valerie Caraotta

When reading through this e-book I was thinking what a great gift it would make for those new to the Lord or in need of Christ. Author Maxwell Kobina Acquah has condensed the Bible theme into a reading that can be done in 1-2 hours. The highlights in the book cover the following:

~ God's initial creation and intention for man
~ man's rebellion and sin
~ God's need to judge His creation through the flood
~ God's grace and desire for you to live for Him.

The Scriptures are numerous and wonderfully listed where the reader can gain clarity on each of these topics discussed. Like the title states there is a condition and man must be mindful of the free will given and how disobedience can block blessings. Acquah understands we live in a fallen world and it doesn't mean all will be well accepting Christ. He does however solidify that God is for us and that there are blessings and benefits to living for Him. At the end of the book is a prayer of salvation.

This author has also credentials as a teacher, minister and motivational speaker. His travels and experiences have allotted him opportunities to share Christ while also clarifying and teaching applicable principles for daily living. I recommend this book and encourage you to explore his other fine books.

Reviewed by   Valerie Caraotta - E-mail: vcar1@juno.com
Phone: 770-922-5310
Spiritually Uplifting, Said by Jacqueline M Piepenhagen

Author, Maxwell Kobina Acquah has put his heart and soul into his first book titled, THERE IS A CONDITION. Who knew that this short book would be filled with such positive feedback for the reader that is looking to find his or her way to God?

In the first chapter titled, THE FIRST LIFE ON EARTH ACCORDING TO THE BIBLE the author writes of the beginning when God created Heaven, earth and man.

He continues on in the second chapter, THE TEN COMMANDMENTS/LAWS and then moves on into chapter three with GOD PROVIDES WITH A CONDITION.

In chapter four, JESUS LOVES YOU, he continues to breakdown the meaning of the verses into layman's terms, then ends with chapter five, YOUR SINS ARE NOT MUCH.

After reading this book I feel it has been appropriately named. This book is not preachy. I found it enlightening and spiritually rewarding. The author explains in an open minded way what God's intent is for each of us. The author walks us through the different chapters and verses from the Bible leaving us with an easy understandable version.

This would be a good book for all age groups to help with guidance and reassurance when life becomes a burden.

This is the first of four books of a series that is now available.

Review by Jacqueline M Piepenhagen -
www.linkedin.com/pub/jacqueline-
piepenhagen/71/27/925
Advice for Contacting Jacqueline
jmpiep@artistofthequill.com
www.facebook.com/jacqueline.piepenhagen.9
www.artistofthequill.com
jackiPiepenhagen@artist_quill

ACKNOWLEDGEMENTS

This book wouldn't have been produced without the help of these great people.

Millicent Adjoa Acquah – Edited the grammar

Robert Thompson (MA, Religious studies, and MDiv) – Adviser and proof reader

Jacob Kwame Afful – Proof reader.

Enock Kojo Ayensu – Proof reader.

Kwame Agyekum – Words of encouragement.

Roland Minnow Afful – Words of encouragement.

Lecturers and Students of American Bible University, and Abundant Life Ministerial Institute, Ghana campus.

James Paakwesi Arthur – Designer.

DEDICATION

I dedicate this book to all believers in CHRIST JESUS.

TABLE OF CONTENTS

INTRODUCTION

The struggle of life begins at birth, simply because of disobedient. Mankind have tried and is still trying to find answers to difficulties in life. People are seeking peace but finding none.

One thing people have forgotten is that the source of life can only be found in God and hence all burdens must be cast unto Him *Psalm 55:2 -Attend unto me, and hear me: I mourn in my complaint, and make a noise;*

GOD is not limited but man is limited. No one has stayed on earth for more than thousand (1000) years, generations have come and gone, people come and go, but God still lives and will live forever. He is the source of life *Genesis 1:25 – 28; 1:25 And God made the beast of the earth after his kind, and cattle after their kind, and every thing that creepeth upon the earth after his kind: and God saw that it was good.*

1:26   And God said, Let us make man in our image, after our likeness: and let them have dominion over the fish of the sea, and over the fowl of the air, and over the cattle, and over all the earth, and over every creeping thing that creepeth upon the earth.

1:27   So God created man in his own image, in the image of God created he him; male and female created he them.

1:28   And God blessed them, and God said unto them, Be fruitful, and multiply, and replenish the earth, and subdue it: and have dominion over the fish of the sea, and over the fowl of the air, and over every living thing that moveth upon the earth.

1:29   And God said, Behold, I have given you every herb bearing seed, which is upon the face of all the earth, and every tree, in the which is the fruit of a tree yielding seed; to you it shall be for meat.

1:30   And to every beast of the earth, and to every fowl of the air, and to every thing that creepeth upon the earth, wherein there is life, I have given every green herb for meat: and it was so.

The Bible has made it clear that he who believes in GOD shall not perish but have eternal life. Matthew 6:33 but seek ye first the Kingdom of GOD, and His righteousness; and all these things shall be added unto you.

The key principle of success is ‚*do unto others what you want others to do unto you'* – *Matthew 7:12.*
This book outlines biblical principles of life.

CHAPTER ONE (1)

THE FIRST LIFE ON EARTH ACCORDING TO THE BIBLE

(The Condition in the Garden of Eden)

According to the Bible after God had created the Heavens and Earth, He created man in His image and placed them in the Garden of Eden. Genesis chapter one gives an account in creation of all things and Chapter two accounts for creation of man.

The image of God as man does not mean man resemble God in complexion, shape, height, weight, and all the features of man, but it rather means that God created man holy, sinless as God is. I remember some time ago in April, 2013 when I was teaching in a private senior high school (Commercial Service Institute – CSI) in Cape Coast, Ghana, where one female student asked me *"sir is GOD white or black, because the Bible says He created man like Himself"* the answer I gave was simple – I answered it in a form of question, *I politely asked her and the class what is the colour*

1

of a black person's and a white person's blood?
The questioner (the female student) said, the colour
of a black person's blood and white person's blood
is the same (red). And I said that's the answer to
your question. *God is colourless, He is a spirit and
He can appear to man in any colour as in the case
of the birth of our Lord and saviour JESUS
CHRIST.* Saved people are one in Christ no matter
where you come from or your colour.

Galatians 3:26-28;

*3:26 For ye are all the children of God by faith in
       Christ Jesus.*

*3:27 For as many of you as have been baptized
       into Christ have put on Christ.*

*3:28 There is neither Jew nor Greek, there is
       neither bond nor free, there is neither male
       nor female: for ye are all one in Christ
       Jesus.*

Romans 12:4-6;

*12:4 For as we have many members in one body,
       and all members have not the same office:*

12:5   So we, being many, are one body in Christ, and every one members one of another.

12:6   Having then gifts differing according to the grace that is given to us, whether prophecy, let us prophesy according to the proportion of faith;

1Corinthians12:4-30;

12:4   Now there are diversities of gifts, but the same Spirit.

12:5   And there are differences of administrations, but the same Lord.

12:6   And there are diversities of operations, but it is the same God which worketh all in all.

12:7   But the manifestation of the Spirit is given to every man to profit withal.

12:8   For to one is given by the Spirit the word of wisdom; to another the word of knowledge by the same Spirit;

12:9   To another faith by the same Spirit; to another the gifts of healing by the same Spirit;

12:10 *To another the working of miracles; to another prophecy; to another discerning of spirits; to another divers kinds of tongues; to another the interpretation of tongues:*

12:11 *But all these worketh that one and the selfsame Spirit, dividing to every man severally as he will.*

12:12 *For as the body is one, and hath many members, and all the members of that one body, being many, are one body: so also is Christ.*

12:13 *For by one Spirit are we all baptized into one body, whether we be Jews or Gentiles, whether we be bond or free; and have been all made to drink into one Spirit.*

12:14 *For the body is not one member, but many.*

12:15 *If the foot shall say, Because I am not the hand, I am not of the body; is it therefore not of the body?*

12:16 *And if the ear shall say, Because I am not the eye, I am not of the body; is it therefore not of the body?*

4

12:17 *If the whole body were an eye, where were the hearing? If the whole were hearing, where were the smelling?*

12:18 *But now hath God set the members every one of them in the body, as it hath pleased him.*

12:19 *And if they were all one member, where were the body?*

12:20 *But now are they many members, yet but one body.*

12:21 *And the eye cannot say unto the hand, I have no need of thee: nor again the head to the feet, I have no need of you.*

12:22 *Nay, much more those members of the body, which seem to be more feeble, are necessary:*

12:23 *And those members of the body, which we think to be less honourable, upon these we bestow more abundant honour; and our uncomely parts have more abundant comeliness.*

12:24 *For our comely parts have no need: but God hath tempered the body together, having* given more abundant honour to that part which lacked:

12:25 That there should be no schism in the body; but that the members should have the same care one for another.

12:26 And whether one member suffer, all the members suffer with it; or one member be honoured, all the members rejoice with it.

12:27 Now ye are the body of Christ, and members in particular.

12:28 And God hath set some in the church, first apostles, secondarily prophets, thirdly teachers, after that miracles, then gifts of healings, helps, governments, diversities of tongues.

12:29 Are all apostles? are all prophets? are all teachers? are all workers of miracles?

12:30 Have all the gifts of healing? do all speak with tongues? do all interpret?

Ephesians 4:11-13.

4:11   *And he gave some, apostles; and some, prophets; and some, evangelists; and some, pastors and teachers;*

4:12   *For the perfecting of the saints, for the work of the ministry, for the edifying of the body of Christ:*

4:13   *Till we all come in the unity of the faith, and of the knowledge of the Son of God, unto a perfect man, unto the measure of the stature of the fullness of Christ:*

So Adam and Eve were perfect, they did not know what sin is and the effects of it, these features represent the image the Bible refers to. God does not sin and do not like sin, He is holy and perfect.

Originally, God gave man power over all creatures He has made, Genesis 1:28-30, but there was a condition attached to that freedom and power over all things God has created.

Genesis 1:28-30;

1:28   And God blessed them, and God said unto them, Be fruitful, and multiply, and replenish the earth, and subdue it: and have dominion over the fish of the sea, and over the fowl of the air, and over every living thing that moveth upon the earth.

1:29   And God said, Behold, I have given you every herb bearing seed, which is upon the face of all the earth, and every tree, in the which is the fruit of a tree yielding seed; to you it shall be for meat.

1:30   And to every beast of the earth, and to every fowl of the air, and to every thing that creepethupon the earth, wherein there is life, I have given every green herb for meat: and it was so.

In Genesis 2:15-17,God asked man not to touch nor eat the fruit of good and evil, if they do, they shall surely die. This is the condition attached to the free will and power God gave over all things. One would ask, if God is Alpha and Omega, all knowing, and not limited why has He attached conditions to man's power over all creatures? The answer is

8

simple – Because God does not want to control man like a robot that is why he gave man the free will of choice. Another question one would also ask is that, how could Satan deceive man? Because the power he was originally given by God when he was in God's Kingdom, was still within him after he had been thrown out from Heaven. „***God does not take back gifts He gives to people, but you cannot use that gift to fight against Him'*** that's why Satan could still operate, but he will be condemned finally at the judgment day. Adam and Eve were affected by what I called „*the WWH factors' – when, where and how.* These led them to obey Satan rather than the Almighty God. Satan capitalised on their free will God had given to them. He approached Eve by asking her questions of the conditionality GOD had given to them. Satan is very intelligent, he knew that Adam will be very difficult to be deceived that is why he approached Eve; (why did he choose Eve), Genesis 3 gives an account to this. Adam and Eve did not know ***where, when and how*** possible they will die if they disobey God Almighty. But they did die in spirit when they ate the fruit of good and evil.

Genesis 2:15 – 17;

2:15   *And the LORD God took the man, and put him into the garden of Eden to dress it and to keep it.*

2:16   *And the LORD God commanded the man, saying, Of every tree of the garden thou mayest freely eat:*

2:17   *But of the tree of the knowledge of good and evil, thou shalt not eat of it: for in the day that thou eatest thereof thou shalt surely die.*

The difference between Lucifer's sin and man's sin is that, Lucifer's sin is from within, he had no external forces (pride and heart desire to over throw GOD Almighty) Job 1:6-12; Zechariah 3:1. But man had an external force who is Satan Genesis 3.

There was a reward for Adam and Eve if they could have obeyed GOD, Genesis 3:22-24, fruit of life (eternal life) was the reward that they would have been awarded with if they have waited. But because of disobedience Adam and Eve were banished from their original home "the Garden of Eden" and thrown outside. So the question to answer is "where is Garden of Eden"? Garden of Eden is different world and is not the same world we are in now according to **Genesis 3:22-24.** -*And the LORD God said, Behold, the man is become as one of us, to know good and evil: and now, lest he put forth his hand, and take also of the tree of life, and eat, and live for ever: 23 Therefore the LORD God sent him forth from the garden of Eden, to till the ground from whence he was taken. 24 So he drove out the man; and he placed at the east of the garden of Eden Cherubims, and a flaming sword which turned every way, to keep the way of the tree of life.*

How is this applicable today? It is applicable today in the Biblical principles that we are to yield to God only and not to disobey Him, for if we disobey Him our blessings would be blocked. There is no perfectness outside the Garden of Eden, where we are now is the world full of conflict, diseases and sickness, hatred, etc. but to those us who believe in the son there is hope for a reward of eternal life and even success in life on this earth before the everlasting life.

Life Outside The Garden Of Eden
In Genesis 3:24 GOD drove Adam and Eve out from the Garden of Eden and placed mighty angels

to guard there. Adam and Eve were cursed Genesis 3:15-19, the man will sweat before getting end means whilst the woman will feel pains in her delivery. All these sufferings were to be effected outside the Garden; this tells us that in the Garden of Eden there is no suffering, death, hunger, hatred, conflict, and so on, there is perfectness and holiness in the Garden of Eden. Once again where is the Garden of Eden? Some are saying it can be located in Ethiopia. Where Eden is have been answered in Genesis 3:24, - unknown, is a world on its own. What you have to understand is you are in a place where there is no perfectness and holiness.

Genesis 3:15-19

3:15   *And I will put enmity between thee and the woman, and between thy seed and her seed; it shall bruise thy head, and thou shalt bruise his heel.*

3:16   *Unto the woman he said, I will greatly multiply thy sorrow and thy conception; in sorrow thou shalt bring forth children; and thy desire shall be to thy husband, and he shall rule over thee.*

12

3:17   *And unto Adam he said, Because thou hast
        hearkened unto the voice of thy wife, and
        hast eaten of the tree, of which I commanded
        thee, saying, Thou shalt not eat of it: cursed
        is the ground for thy sake; in sorrow shalt
        thou eat of it all the days of thy life;*

3:18   *Thorns also and thistles shall it bring forth
        to thee; and thou shalt eat the herb of the
        field;*

3:19   *In the sweat of thy face shalt thou eat bread,
        till thou return unto the ground; for out of it
        wast thou taken: for dust thou art, and unto
        dust shalt thou return.*

In Genesis 4, Adam laid (slept) with his wife and
gave birth to Cain and later gave birth to a second
son Abel. These two sons grew up and Cain became
a farmer (crops farmer) and Abel became a
shepherd (animal farmer). In the process it came to
pass that they are to offer sacrifices to God at their
harvest time. Cain the elder son, brought to God the
fruit of the ground (unattractive vegetables) whilst
Abel the younger son brought to God the firstlings
of his flock and of the fat thereof. God rejected
Cain's offering and accepted that of Abel. Cain did

13

not willingly give from his heart but his younger brother Abel did gave willingly from his heart. Cain killed his brother because of jealousy and God got angry of him. Cain was banished from the land to another land. Cain could not follow the principles of obedience and hence he suffered all the consequences of disobeying God. All these things happened in this present earth we are currently in, outside the Garden of Eden.

In the case of Cain and Abel, it is applicable today. Many people have the perception that the offertory or the tithes they give in the Church is for the pastor so they do not give willingly from their heart. A lot of people refuse to give to support God's work yet they want to be blessed. God blesses those who willingly offer sacrifice of worship. Giving, supporting, actively participating in God's are all forms of worship. In Luke 21:1-4 the widow willingly gave from her heart unlike the rich man who did not. Exodus 35:21-29; Malachi 3:8-10; Luke 6:38; Leviticus 27:30.

What we have to understand is that there is no free lunch. Everything comes with a condition, but the conditions from God avoid hatred, conflict, war, discrimination, diseases and sickness, and all sufferings of life. God does not plan evil for man but Lucifer does plan evil and destruction for man, John 10:10.

Notably people seek magical powers to enrich themselves, for political power, and so many worldly things. Even these artificial powers people seek come with conditions which they try to obey. If people can obey conditions attached to these limited powers why don't they obey God who is the source of life to have a comfortable everlasting life?

The Bible says, seek ye first the kingdom of God and His righteousness and the blessings shall be added unto you. So the condition is to ***seek first the Kingdom of God and His righteousness*** for blessing, without yielding to God your blessings will be blocked; Matthew 6:33 - 34; 2:3 1Sammuel 9:20; Mark 4:18-19; Ecclesiastes 11:10.

Noah And The Flood (Conditions To Be Saved)

Noah is the son of Seth and grandson of Adam and Eve, Genesis 5. The population on earth increased in Noah's era (generation) and wickedness also increased. God warned mankind through Noah His servant. But the people wouldn't listen to Noah and continued to sinned, Genesis 6.

Noah was the only righteous man living on earth by then. He consistently obeyed God's will and did not follow the world. God said to Noah, „because the people have become corrupt and do not obey me, I will destroy the earth'. „Make a boat from *resinous wood* and seal it with *tar*, inside and outside',

Genesis 6:14-16;

14 Make thee an ark of gopher wood; rooms shalt thou make in the ark, and shalt pitch it within and without with pitch.

15 And this is the fashion which thou shalt make it of: The length of the ark shall be three hundred cubits, the breadth of it fifty cubits, and the height of it thirty cubits.

16 A window shalt thou make to the ark, and in a cubit shalt thou finish it above; and the door of

16

the ark shalt thou set in the side thereof; with lower, second, and third stories shalt thou make it.

Here there was a command "***make a boat***". God promised Noah not to destroy him, "but he should make a boat". So the question is "if Noah had not obeyed God, what would have happened to him and his family? Genesis 7, Noah obeyed the condition given to him and he and the family and even the animals were saved. How does this imply to you?
Do you obey God's word?
Are you of Christ or of the world?
How prepared are you if Christ comes today?
As for Noah and his family they were of God and ready for Him and were saved, Genesis 8.
Are you fulfilling the conditions of following Christ? 1Timothy 3:1 - 16 and Galatians 5:1 – 26.
Noah followed God; he obeyed the principles, worshipped God from his heart.

Man is created to worship and not to be worshipped. The people in Noah's generation did not obey God and were destroyed.

17

Proverbs 6:16 – 21

6:16 These six things doth the LORD hate: yea, seven are an abomination unto him:

6:17 A proud look, a lying tongue, and hands that shed innocent blood,

6:18 An heart that deviseth wicked imaginations, feet that be swift in running to mischief,

6:19 A false witness that speaketh lies, and he that soweth discord among brethren.

6:20 My son, keep thy father's commandment, and forsake not the law of thy mother:

6:21 Bind them continually upon thine heart, and tie them about thy neck.

John 14:15- *If ye love me, keep my commandments.*

CHAPTER TWO (2)

THE TEN COMMANDMENTS/LAW

Exodus Chapter 20:1 - 17

20:1   And God spake all these words, saying,

20:2   I am the LORD thy God, which have brought thee out of the land of Egypt, out of the house of bondage.

20:3   Thou shalt have no other gods before me.

20:4   Thou shalt not make unto thee any graven image, or any likeness of any thing that is in heaven above, or that is in the earth beneath, or that is in the water under the earth:

20:5   Thou shalt not bow down thyself to them, nor serve them: for I the LORD thy God am a jealous God, visiting the iniquity of the fathers upon the children unto the third and fourth generation of them that hate me;

20:6   And showing mercy unto thousands of them that love me, and keep my commandments.

20:7   *Thou shalt not take the name of the LORD thy God in vain; for the LORD will not hold him guiltless that taketh his name in vain.*

20:8   *Remember the sabbath day, to keep it holy.*

20:9   *Six days shalt thou labour, and do all thy work:*

20:10   *But the seventh day is the sabbath of the LORD thy God: in it thou shalt not do any work, thou, nor thy son, nor thy daughter, thy manservant, nor thy maidservant, nor thy cattle, nor thy stranger that is within thy gates:*

20:11   *For in six days the LORD made heaven and earth, the sea, and all that in them is, and rested the seventh day: wherefore the LORD blessed the sabbath day, and hallowed it.*

20:12   *Honour thy father and thy mother: that thy days may be long upon the land which the LORD thy God giveth thee.*

20:13   *Thou shalt not kill.*

20:14   *Thou shalt not commit adultery.*

20:15   *Thou shalt not steal.*

20:16 Thou shalt not bear false witness against thy neighbour.

20:17 Thou shalt not covet thy neighbour's house, thou shalt not covet thy neighbour's wife, nor his manservant, nor his maidservant, nor his ox, nor his ass, nor any thing that is thy neighbour's.

Deuteronomy 5:7-16

5:7 Thou shalt have none other gods before me.

5:8 Thou shalt not make thee any graven image, or any likeness of any thing that is in heaven above, or that is in the earth beneath, or that is in the waters beneath the earth:

5:9 Thou shalt not bow down thyself unto them, nor serve them: for I the LORD thy God am a jealous God, visiting the iniquity of the fathers upon the children unto the third and fourth generation of them that hate me,

5:10 And showing mercy unto thousands of them that love me and keep my commandments.

5:11 *Thou shalt not take the name of the LORD thy God in vain: for the LORD will not hold him guiltless that taketh his name in vain.*

5:12 *Keep the sabbath day to sanctify it, as the LORD thy God hath commanded thee.*

5:13 *Six days thou shalt labour, and do all thy work:*

5:14 *But the seventh day is the sabbath of the LORD thy God: in it thou shalt not do any work, thou, nor thy son, nor thy daughter, nor thy manservant, nor thy maidservant, nor thine ox, nor thine ass, nor any of thy cattle, nor thy stranger that is within thy gates; that thy manservant and thy maidservant may rest as well as thou.*

5:15 *And remember that thou wast a servant in the land of Egypt, and that the LORD thy God brought thee out thence through a mighty hand and by a stretched out arm: therefore the LORD thy God commanded thee to keep the sabbath day.*

5:16 *Honour thy father and thy mother, as the LORD thy God hath commanded thee; that thy days may be prolonged, and that it may go well with thee, in the land which the LORD thy God giveth thee.*

Deuteronomy 5: 17 - 22

5:17 Thou shalt not kill.

5:18 Neither shalt thou commit adultery.

5:19 Neither shalt thou steal.

5:20 Neither shalt thou bear false witness against thy neighbour.

5:21 Neither shalt thou desire thy neighbour's wife, neither shalt thou covet thy neighbour's house, his field, or his manservant, or his maidservant, his ox, or his ass, or any thing that is thy neighbour's.

5:22 These words the LORD spake unto all your assembly in the mount out of the midst of the fire, of the cloud, and of the thick darkness, with a great voice: and he added no more. And he wrote them in two tables of stone, and delivered them unto me.

Exodus 34:1 *And the LORD said unto Moses, Hew thee two tables of stone like unto the first:*

and I will write upon these tables the words that were in the first tables, which thou brakest.

Applicable or Not

To some influential and non - influential pastors and other people, the Ten Commandments are not applicable in our generation because it is by grace we are saved. Should we obey some parts of the Bible and reject some? Some people believe in only the Old Testament and others believe in only the New Testament. It is true that salvation is by grace through faith alone and not by works but there is a condition, which is the Ten Commandments. Man cannot have salvation without recognising the Ten Commandments.

JESUS said in Matthew 5:17-20;

17 Think not that I am come to destroy the law, or the prophets: I am not come to destroy, but to fulfil.

18 For verily I say unto you, Till heaven and earth pass, one jot or one title shall in no wise pass from the law, till all be fulfilled.

24

19 *Whosoever therefore shall break one of these least commandments, and shall teach men so, he shall be called the least in the kingdom of heaven: but whosoever shall do and teach them, the same shall be called great in the kingdom of heaven.*

20 *For I say unto you, That except your righteousness shall exceed the righteousness of the scribes and Pharisees, ye shall in no case enter into the kingdom of heaven.*

From the above Bible quotations, Jesus is clear about the effects of the Law. I remember in May, 2013 I read a comment by one of my face book friends asking and I quote *"when was the Bible written?"* my answer to that question was difficult for some people to understand but simple – I said, the Bible was written right from the day of creation, John 1:1-5, *verse 1 - in the beginning was the Word, and the Word was with God, and the Word was God*. Who is the word? Jesus is the word. What is the Law? The law is Jesus Christ – John 14:15, says *if ye love me, keep my commandments*. What commandments is Jesus referring to? The commandment is the Bible, not Pharisees law or

25

man's law or any twisted religious teachings. The Ten Commandments have been summed up in JESUS CHRIST. If you love JESUS you will not kill, gossip, create conflict, worship other gods, and all the immoralities listed in Galatians 5. Amongst the Ten Commandments the greatest of all is *love* and love can be found in Jesus Christ. Some people limit God by disregarding what God demands from us. Man was created to glorify God. God is not limited like man or other gods, He is the source of life and the beginning and the end. What people need to understand is that, the Ten Commandments have been summed up in LOVE. The Ten Commandments is applicable even unto this day. Obey it to receive Heavenly power.

A definition of the Christian doctrine of salvation would be "The deliverance, by the grace of God, from eternal punishment for sin which is granted to those who accept by faith God's conditions of repentance and faith in the Lord Jesus." Salvation is available in Jesus alone (John 14:6; Acts 4:12) and is dependent on God alone for provision, assurance, and security.

The Law of God

The law is true – Psalm 119:142–151;
Perfect – Psalm 19:7; James 1:25;
Trustworthy – Psalm 19:7; 119:86, 138
Enduring – Psalm 119:91, 160; Matthew 5:18.
Right and righteous – Psalm 19:8; 137; Romans 7:12
Holy – Romans 7:12
Good – Romans 7:12, 16; 1Timothy 1:8
Spiritual – Romans 7:14

Love is its summary – Matthew 22:37-40; Romans 13:8-10; Galatians 5:14.

All the above are the characteristics of the law of GOD. Please the law I am stressing on is not the ceremonial or cultural or Israelites or any other religious or man-made law but the Bible. The Bible is the law book and that is what I am referring to and not any other book. The Ten Commandment is part of the whole law book – *THE BIBLE.* Love is the summary of all the laws and the greatest of all in the Ten Commandments. So the key principle is *love* which can be found in Jesus Christ.

As I have already said, Jesus Christ is the commandments – John 14:15 and the commandments is the word and the word is the law which guides man to the Father – John 14:6. The condition is that no one can enter into God's Kingdom without recognising Jesus Christ as Lord and personal saviour. The Bible is a salvation manual that we ought to read and implement its principles in our daily life. No one can claim to be righteous without obeying the Bible. I am fully aware that once we in the world of imperfectness certain life conditions may try to force us to make mistakes in life but that mistake should not lead you away from Jesus. Jesus knows our weaknesses, and will not let us down when we yield to Him, just read the book of Job, upon all that he went through he did never turned his back to God. Challenges may arise but because of Christ in you the hope of glory.

The Fulfilment of the Law

As discussed in the beginning of this chapter, Jesus in Matthew 5:17-20 said; He did not come to destroy the law but to fulfil it. The law was a shadow of the things to come – the Old Testament was the shadow of the New Testament. All the prophecies about the birth and life of the messiah, the end time, and many things were recorded in the Old Testament. Jesus came to fulfil whatever was said by the prophets – the New Testament confirms the Old Testament, John 15:25 – 27; 1Corinthians 14:21. Those who say that neither the Old Testament nor the Ten Commandment is applicable today are in error. Those have forgotten that the coming of the messiah was prophesied and the greatest amongst the Ten Commandments is love.

Matthew 22:37-40; (*37 Jesus said unto him, Thou shalt love the Lord thy God with all thy heart, and with all thy soul, and with all thy mind. 38 This is the first and great commandment. 39 And the second is like unto it, Thou shalt love thy neighbour as thyself. 40 On these two commandments hang all the law and the prophets*) fulfils the Ten Commandments. It makes it clear that love God with your heart, love your neighbour as yourself. These summaries the Biblical principles or the laws recorded by the prophets – Galatians 5:14; Romans 13:8-10. The condition is that hates sin and love good things. Jesus fulfils the law in the New Testament, so do not ignore the Old Testament teachings, they are applicable.

CHAPTER THREE (3)

GOD PROVIDES WITH A CONDITION

In Matthew 7:7, God says we should ***ask, seek, and knock***, and He will answer us, then in Matthew 6:9-12, we petition God to protect us, provide our daily meals to us and forgive us our sins. Many people forget the conditions attached to these provisions.

Matthew 7:7-12

7 *Ask, and it shall be given you; seek, and ye shall find; knock, and it shall be opened unto you:*

8 *For every one that asketh receiveth; and he that seeketh findeth; and to him that knocketh it shall be opened.*

9 *Or what man is there of you, whom if his son ask bread, will he give him a stone?*

10 *Or if he ask a fish, will he give him a serpent?*

11 *If ye then, being evil, know how to give good gifts unto your children, how much more shall your Father which is in heaven give good things to them that ask him?*

30

12 Therefore all things whatsoever ye would that men should do to you, do ye even so to them: for this is the law and the prophets.

The condition attached to the petition in Matthew 7:1 – 12, is *,do unto others what you want others to do unto you'*, this is found in verse 12. People ignore this particular verse which is a condition attached to the petition. This condition means you reap what you sow. God answers prayers of a repented heart. If you don't show love, kindness, etc. God will also not answer you. One needs to examine himself or herself before petitioning God. God is always ready to forgive the repented heart. Do unto others what you want others to do unto you is what is referred to as the *Golden Rule – this is a summary of all the taught in the law and the prophets.*

Matthew 6:9-15
9   After this manner therefore pray ye: Our Father which art in heaven, Hallowed be thy name.

10   Thy kingdom come. Thy will be done in earth, as it is in heaven.

31

11   Give us this day our daily bread.

12   And forgive us our debts, as we forgive our debtors.

13   And lead us not into temptation, but deliver us from evil: For thine is the kingdom, and the power, and the glory, for ever. Amen.

14   For if ye forgive men their trespasses, your heavenly Father will also forgive you:

15   But if ye forgive not men their trespasses, neither will your Father forgive your trespasses.

There is a condition attached to the model prayer (the Lord's Prayer). Matthew 6:9-13, 14, in verse 12 the condition is if you do not forgive others who have sinned against you, you will also not be forgiving. Just ask yourself if you have forgiving the one who offended you. Many people prayers are not answered because they are ignorant about this. The verse 14 explains further the condition.

Most people contradict themselves in petitioning God, that's why their prayers are not answered. If you steal to enrich yourself, someone will also steal from you, if you sleep with somebody's wife or husband the same will be done to you. Whatever you do to others, the same will be done to you – says the Bible, which is our law book. Please Jesus is ready to forgive you all your sins, you did not know, just come to Him with a repented heart.

A typical example of this condition is in the case of King David, when he slept with one of his soldiers' wife, even though he pleaded for forgiveness of his sins after Nathan had confronted him of what he has done, he still suffered the consequences „his own son – Amnon, slept with his own sister Tamar and a lot happened in his family' 2Samuel 13. That does not mean God did not accept his pleadings, but God wanted David to recognise the pains he caused the man and the family went through, so that he will use it to advice others not to do the same. Read the full story in 2 Samuel chapters 11 and 12, and pleadings in Psalm 51.

If you have repented and still going through some challenges please do not think that God has not forgiving you your sins, what you are going through is temporary, keep on looking unto God, He is the source of eternal life and your problems are nothing that He cannot do, H is more than able to do away with every problem.

Be Real (Genuine)
In this world you have to be real, follow principles. God has giving man the will of free choice. You can choose to follow God or the other side, but I prefer you follow God. Do not waver between hot and cold, if you want to be hot be hot, if you want to be cold be cold.

In 2 Timothy 2:22, *Flee also youthful lusts: but follow righteousness, faith, charity, peace, with them that call on the Lord out of a pure heart.*

Matthew 6:33, *But seek ye first the kingdom of God, and his righteousness; and all these things shall be added unto you.*

1KINGS 3:3-15
3:3   *And Solomon loved the LORD, walking in the statutes of David his father: only he sacrificed and burnt incense in high places.*

3:4   *And the king went to Gibeon to sacrifice there; for that was the great high place: a thousand burnt offerings did Solomon offer upon that altar.*

3:5   *In Gibeon the LORD appeared to Solomon in a dream by night: and God said, Ask what I shall give thee.*

3:6   *And Solomon said, Thou hast showed unto thy servant David my father great mercy, according as he walked before thee in truth, and in righteousness, and in uprightness of heart with thee; and thou hast kept for him this great kindness, that thou hast given him a son to sit on his throne, as it is this day.*

3:7   *And now, O LORD my God, thou hast made thy servant king instead of David my father: and I am but a little child: I know not how to go out or come in.*

3:8   *And thy servant is in the midst of thy people which thou hast chosen, a great people, that cannot be numbered nor counted for multitude.*

3:9   *Give therefore thy servant an understanding heart to judge thy people, that I may discern between good and bad: for who is able to judge this thy so great a people?*

3:10 *And the speech pleased the Lord, that Solomon had asked this thing.*

3:11 *And God said unto him, Because thou hast asked this thing, and hast not asked for thyself long life; neither hast asked riches for thyself, nor hast asked the life of thine enemies; but hast asked for thyself understanding to discern judgment;*

3:12 *Behold, I have done according to thy words: lo, I have given thee a wise and an understanding heart; so that there was none like thee before thee, neither after thee shall any arise like unto thee.*

3:13 *And I have also given thee that which thou hast not asked, both riches, and honour: so that there shall not be any among the kings like unto thee all thy days.*

3:14 *And if thou wilt walk in my ways, to keep my statutes and my commandments, as thy father David did walk, then I will lengthen thy days.*

3:15   *And Solomon awoke; and, behold, it was a dream. And he came to Jerusalem, and stood before the ark of the covenant of the LORD, and offered up burnt offerings, and offered peace offerings, and made a feast to all his servants.*

In 1Kings 3:3-15, Solomon asked for wisdom and God blessed him. What are you asking for? Is it better marriage, money, good work, good education, political power or what? Let Solomon be your example in your prayers, ask for wisdom, seek first the Kingdom of God and its righteousness and be bless abundantly, 2Chronicles 1:2-13; Isaiah 30:15. Elijah, Jeremiah, Moses, and all the prophets and apostles were just human beings like me and you. Let's have the desire to seek first the Kingdom of God and its righteousness in truth and in spirit for GOD to bless us. Yield to God only, He is the Alpha and Omega, the Beginner and ender of life. Ask God to give you power, courage to do His will, He is the source of life and loves us all.

Do not let your past to worry you in worshipping God. Recognise Jesus Christ once and for all in your life.

CHAPTER FOUR (4)

JESUS LOVES YOU

In John 3:16; *(For God so loved the world, that he gave his only begotten Son, that whosoever believeth in him should not perish, but have everlasting life)* Genesis 15:6; Habakkuk 2:4; Acts 16:30-31, God loves you that is why He made provision for salvation when man was thrown out of the Garden of Eden. He sent His only begotten son to come and bridge the gap between God and man. God needs you back because He created you and loves you. He has provided the way to you, and the way is Jesus Christ – John 14:6.

Jesus is right at your door calling you to open so that he can enter, it is your choice, He is not forcing you because of the free will of choice He has giving you. God is speaking through me and other men or people of God to tell you to change. Jesus said, in His teachings that He is ready to forgive the repented heart. He will come for those who love Him. He is preparing a beautiful place where there wouldn't be conflict, war, diseases and sickness,

38

poverty, and so on, the place would be perfect and holy and only the repented heart will enter there. Just yield to JESUS, have faith and believe in the Bible.

Do not ask God who is He, and when did He came into existence, and how does He works, and so on but just believe that He is the Almighty God who does what He want without anyone's permission.

Recognise JESUS as the Law

In Matthew 10:33, Jesus said *But whosoever shall deny me before men, him will I also deny before my Father which is in heaven,* Luke 12:9; 2Timothy 2:12. If you feel shy in proclaiming the gospel wherever you are and whoever you come across with, JESUS will also feel shy of you. Your lifestyle alone can influence others to God. You need not to be giving the pulpit before evangelising; evangelism can take place in anywhere and many ways, in school, workplace, online preaching or internet, text messages, in your dressing, your associates friends, and many places and ways in different biblical methods.

JESUS is the law that we are to obey. If you recognise JESUS in your life, JESUS will also recognise you. Salvation is not a free lunch, it comes with a condition, the condition is to deny the world and accept JESUS CHRIST as Lord and Saviour.

CHAPTER FIVE (5)

YOUR SINS ARE NOT MUCH

In chapter one through to chapter four of this book, you have read about what happened in the Garden of Eden and its consequences. God being all knowing God, He had a purpose for man. He is not limited and has power over all things.

Luke 19:1-10

1   *And Jesus entered and passed through Jericho.*

2   *And, behold, there was a man named Zacchaeus, which was the chief among the publicans, and he was rich.*

3   *And he sought to see Jesus who he was; and could not for the press, because he was little of stature.*

4   *And he ran before, and climbed up into a sycamore tree to see him: for he was to pass that way.*

5   *And when Jesus came to the place, he looked up, and saw him, and said unto him,*

41

Zacchaeus, make haste, and come down; for to day I must abide at thy house.

6 *And he made haste, and came down, and received him joyfully.*

7 *And when they saw it, they all murmured, saying, That he was gone to be guest with a man that is a sinner.*

8 *And Zacchaeus stood, and said unto the Lord; Behold, Lord, the half of my goods I give to the poor; and if I have taken any thing from any man by false accusation, I restore him fourfold.*

9 *And Jesus said unto him, This day is salvation come to this house, forsomuch as he also is a son of Abraham.*

10 *For the Son of man is come to seek and to save that which was lost.*

In Luke 19:1-10, there was a man named Zaccheus, which was the chief among the publicans, and he was rich. He was a sinner, when he head of Jesus he decided to see who really He was because Jesus had been doing wonderful things beyond human understanding. And he, Zaccheus ran to before and climbed up onto a sycomore tree to see Jesus for he was to pass that way. When Jesus got to the place He looked up and saw him and told him Zaccheus make haste and come down for today I must abide at thy house. Zaccheus obeyed Jesus and came down to embrace Jesus. The followers of Christ were shock for Christ to said He shall eat together with such a sinner of sinners.

The application here is that no matter what you have than, Jesus is ready to forgive you your sins only if you will deny the world and follow Him as Zaccheus did. The condition is deny the world, obey the Biblical principles and JESUS will welcome you.

Acts 9:1-15

1   And Saul, yet breathing out threatenings and slaughter against the disciples of the Lord, went unto the high priest,

2   And desired of him letters to Damascus to the synagogues, that if he found any of this way, whether they were men or women, he might bring them bound unto Jerusalem.

3   *And as he journeyed, he came near Damascus: and suddenly there shined round about him a light from heaven:*

4   *And he fell to the earth, and heard a voice saying unto him, Saul, Saul, why persecutest thou me?*

5   *And he said, Who art thou, Lord? And the Lord said, I am Jesus whom thou persecutest: it is hard for thee to kick against the pricks.*

6   *And he trembling and astonished said, Lord, what wilt thou have me to do? And the Lord said unto him, Arise, and go into the city, and it shall be told thee what thou must do.*

7   *And the men which journeyed with him stood speechless, hearing a voice, but seeing no man.*

8   *And Saul arose from the earth; and when his eyes were opened, he saw no man: but they led him by the hand, and brought him into Damascus.*

9   *And he was three days without sight, and neither did eat nor drink.*

10 *And there was a certain disciple at Damascus, named Ananias; and to him said the Lord in a*

vision, Ananias. And he said, Behold, I am here, Lord.

11 And the Lord said unto him, Arise, and go into the street which is called Straight, and inquire in the house of Judas for one called Saul, of Tarsus: for, behold, he prayeth,

12 And hath seen in a vision a man named Ananias coming in, and putting his hand on him, that he might receive his sight.

13 Then Ananias answered, Lord, I have heard by many of this man, how much evil he hath done to thy saints at Jerusalem:

14 And here he hath authority from the chief priests to bind all that call on thy name.

15 But the Lord said unto him, Go thy way: for he is a chosen vessel unto me, to bear my name before the Gentiles, and kings, and the children of Israel:

Paul, who was originally known as Saul, was a very religious person (a Pharisee) and persecuted the followers of Christ who were proclaiming (spreading) the gospel. He led other Pharisees kill the disciples like animals, made them uncomfortable of their mission. He was met by Christ on his way to Damascus and was saved. He denied his false religion and obeyed the principles of Christ. One may say, but he thought initially that his religion is the true religion, so Jesus only showed him the true one; Yes but know that in this world everybody believes in something which there is a belief that there is true Creator that they are worshipping, that true creator can only be found in Jesus only and nothing or one else, John 14:6.

If Paul of all sinners by then was saved by Jesus, know that he was also a human being just like you, your sins are not much come to Jesus, and He is ever ready to forgive you. The conditions are repent of your sins and obey the Bible. Acts 7-9 gives detailed account of Paul, Philippians 3:15; 3:6; Galatians 1:13-14; Acts 9:1-43; 22:6-21; 26:16-18.

You may not be a Christian but in a different religion, you did not know now that you have got to know, deny your religion and come to Christ. Let Paul and Zaccheus be your examples, they realised that they are mistaking, they were ignorant of the truth, but when they got to know the truth, they

46

denied the world (religion) and came to know JESUS CHRIST.

There are many examples in the Bible of people who realised that without Jesus there is no salvation.

I pray in the mighty name of JESUS CHRIST that as you have read this book you will realise that salvation can only be found in JESUS alone by grace and faith in Him.

The GRACE refers to the love, passion, will and readiness of GOD to forgive ones sins.

Faith alone is the work that the person in the process of being saved or have been saved will have in GOD. That's the zeal of recognising GOD as the saviour. And this is the condition, for GOD He is ever ready by His grace.

The Uncertainty of Salvation

There is confusion about the proper definition of salvation, I have already defined it in this book, but I want to make a clear Biblical difference between *once saved ever saved, and once saved not ever saved.* The parable of Jesus on seed sawing defines this very well.

Once saved ever saved refers to a born again Christian who produces the fruit of the spirit. The person may commit some mistakes in life, but I tell you anyone who has the spirit in him, anytime he does something wrong the spirit rebukes him and quickly within him he repents. A good example can be refer to the disciples or apostles, I have not come across any book or verse in the Bible that records that any of them went back after Christ had giving the power to them. Although they may have some disagreement between them on some issues but they did never deny JESUS CHRIST. Ephesians 5:22-23; 4:2-3; Romans 14:17; Colossians 3:12-15; 2Pet. 1:5-7.

Galatians 5:22-26

5:22   But the fruit of the Spirit is love, joy, peace, longsuffering, gentleness, goodness, faith,

5:23   Meekness, temperance: against such there is no law.

5:24   And they that are Christ's have crucified the flesh with the affections and lusts.

5:25   If we live in the Spirit, let us also walk in the Spirit.

5:26 Let us not be desirous of vain glory, provoking one another, envying one another.

Romans 14:17 - *For the kingdom of God is not meat and drink; but righteousness, and peace, and joy in the Holy Ghost.*

Once saved not ever saved refers to a person who is immature in the word, not baptised by the Holy Spirit, wavers between hot and cold, and not feel guilty of wrong doings. A typical example is Judas Iscariot, who betrayed JESUS CHRIST, he was in the process of getting saved but not saved. One may asked, wasn't it his destiny, I will say is a mystery, let the Holy Spirit gives you the answer.

Galatians 5:19 - 21

5:19 Now the works of the flesh are manifest, which are these; Adultery, fornication, uncleanness, lasciviousness,

5:20 Idolatry, witchcraft, hatred, variance, emulations, wrath, strife, seditions, heresies,

5:21 Envyings, murders, drunkenness, revellings, and such like: of the which I tell you before, as I have also told you in time past, that they which do such things shall not inherit the kingdom of God.

The Parable of a Seed Sower
Matthew 13:1-23

13:1 *The same day went Jesus out of the house, and sat by the sea side.*

13:2 *And great multitudes were gathered together unto him, so that he went into a ship, and sat; and the whole multitude stood on the shore.*

13:3 *And he spake many things unto them in parables, saying, Behold, a sower went forth to sow;*

13:4 *And when he sowed, some seeds fell by the way side, and the fowls came and devoured them up:*

13:5 *Some fell upon stony places, where they had not much earth: and forthwith they sprung up, because they had no deepness of earth:*

13:6 *And when the sun was up, they were scorched; and because they had no root, they withered away.*

13:7   And some fell among thorns; and the thorns sprung up, and choked them:

13:8   But other fell into good ground, and brought forth fruit, some an hundredfold, some sixtyfold, some thirtyfold.

13:9   Who hath ears to hear, let him hear.

13:10 And the disciples came, and said unto him, Why speakest thou unto them in parables?

13:11 He answered and said unto them, Because it is given unto you to know the mysteries of the kingdom of heaven, but to them it is not given.

13:12 For whosoever hath, to him shall be given, and he shall have more abundance: but whosoever hath not, from him shall be taken away even that he hath.

13:13 Therefore speak I to them in parables: because they seeing see not; and hearing they hear not, neither do they understand.

13:14 And in them is fulfilled the prophecy of Esaias, which saith, By hearing ye shall hear, and shall not understand; and seeing ye shall see, and shall not perceive:

51

13:15 For this people's heart is waxed gross, and their ears are dull of hearing, and their eyes they have closed; lest at any time they should see with their eyes and hear with their ears, and should understand with their heart, and should be converted, and I should heal them.

13:16 But blessed are your eyes, for they see: and your ears, for they hear.

13:17 For verily I say unto you, That many prophets and righteous men have desired to see those things which ye see, and have not seen them; and to hear those things which ye hear, and have not heard them.

13:18 Hear ye therefore the parable of the sower.

13:19 When any one heareth the word of the kingdom, and understandeth it not, then cometh the wicked one, and catcheth away that which was sown in his heart. This is he which received seed by the way side.

13:20 But he that received the seed into stony places, the same is he that heareth the word, and anon with joy receiveth it;

13:21 Yet hath he not root in himself, but dureth for a while: for when tribulation or persecution ariseth because of the word, by and by he is offended.

13:22 He also that received seed among the thorns is he that heareth the word; and the care of this world, and the deceitfulness of riches, choke the word, and he becometh unfruitful.

13:23 But he that received seed into the good ground is he that heareth the word, and understandeth it; which also beareth fruit, and bringeth forth, some an hundredfold, some sixty, some thirty.

If you are not born again, JESUS is right at your door asking you to open HIM to give you salvation.

Find a well Bible believing Church who believes in the following in JESUS teachings and go.

If your life is NOT right with Jesus Christ/YeshuahHaMashiach or do not know HIM then pray the following prayer from the bottom of your heart:

"Dear GOD the Father, Son and the Holy Spirit, I come to YOU in the wonderful and most POWERFUL name above all names, the name of Jesus Christ/YeshuahHaMashiach. I am a Sinner, come into my heart and redeem me with YOUR POWERFUL Blood and wash me from all sin. Please send YOUR Holy Spirit to lead me and teach me in YOUR ways. Please write my name in the „LAMB's Book of Life'. Thank YOU for protecting me with YOUR POWERFUL blood that was shed on the cross of Calvary. This I pray in YOUR wonderful name, the name of Jesus Christ/YeshuahHaMashiach. Amen!"

Volume two of this book explains into detail the subject of THERE IS A CONDITION.

Criticisms are welcomed through
infoyefulkay@gmail.com

Other Books by the Author

1. Eternity Is Just A Step Across The Threshold.

2. The Church: Is Not What You Think.

3. Life After Death: Where Would You Be If You Die Today?

4. The Downfall of Man is out of WWH

5. The World Leaders and Homosexuality Legalisation, The Secret Behind – volume 1

Contact address of the author
P. O. Box AD 730,
Cape Coast,
Ghana.
www.mkacquah.webs.com/
www.facebook.com/mkacquah
www.facebook.com/yefulkay